Kinetic Spelling
for
Active Learners
K - 4

TINA JACOBS RAMSAY

and

SHANTELL ANDROSCHUK

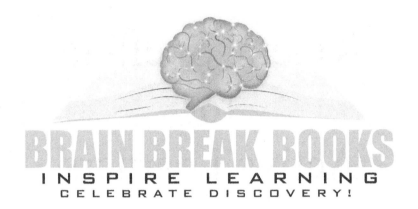

ISBN - 13: 978 - 1976009211

ISBN - 10: 1976009219

DEDICATION

This book is dedicated to our amazing husbands, friends and family who supported our efforts in this venture. Curtis, your love, support and guidance is the stronghold that keeps your family together. Jerry and Carrie; your encouragement and spiritual example have brightened both of our worlds in Canada and the US. Artur and Lori; your enduring support has smoothed many a bumpy road. We may be the Peanut Butter and Jelly but YOU guys are the bread that holds it all together. Thank you.

Most adamantly, we wish to thank the marvellous youngsters that made us mothers and teach us so much every day. You are the embodiment of our hopes and dreams and we thank Jehovah every day for the miracle of YOU.

All the love to Tazhae, Isaiah, Cheridynn, Éowynn, Atticus and Brigette…

Your crazy Mommas love you.

CONTENTS

Dear Parent:

Is your little one a "wiggly" learner? The kind that never seems to stop moving? No need to stress it; just embrace it! Work with their tendencies and use this book to keep the learning fun!

There is an activity listed with each lesson. In many cases, these can make your spelling count for physical education as well. It is likely that your child will beg you to practice their spelling again and again. How often you do is entirely up to you and your child. Show enthusiasm for the lessons and you will find it to be contagious. Rest assured, these words are taken from the lists of most commonly mispelled words in the english language; the learning is real! After each list is a story using the words in sentences. Your child can help find each word and highlight or underline them. The lists get progressively more difficult as it was our intention to build up confidence while also instilling higher level learning.

A helpful hint: Try not to focus on making spelling a pass/fail scenario. The goal is to have the words be learned, not to regurgitate memorized info on a paper at demand. Perhaps when they get a word correct 3 days in a row, you can consider it learned. Create a "Spelling words" binder that they can they can proudly add learned words to. Celebrate when they reach so many words mastered or so many pages filled. An ice cream or trip to a playground is a great memory to associate with the learning of spelling. Feel free to sneak previously learned words into future lessons occasionally just to reinforce the learning.

We would LOVE to hear your thoughts and ideas to add to future editions.

Have fun spelling!

How to Use This Book

Well, it is time to plan out our spelling lessons!

This book is pretty straight forward to use and the strategies are some that we have had to develop to keep our own wiggly littles learning and focused. It is hard to break out of that "desk and chalkboard" mindset, so give yourself some time to wrap your head around it. Some youngsters just need to be moving and that's okay! They learn best in motion so we can certainly help you facilitate that.

There are 15 lessons, each containing 10 spelling words chosen from lists of the most commonly misspelled words in the english language. As most school areas insist upon 36+ weeks of schooling, this allows 2-3 weeks to get through each lesson. Don't stress about doing all 10 words at once. Give only what the child can handle. 2-3 words is plenty for a beginning speller.
Read the words to them letter by letter.

Now practice your words using the kinetic activity listed. Keep the lessons short and fun. Stop before the child is tired of it. Keep them wanting more! 5 or 10 minutes a day of fun is far more effective than an hour of monotonous drills. Once a word is learned, don't keep drilling it. Would you want to keep practicing 2 + 2?…Neither would I. Take time to allow your learner to draw definitions for their words in the boxes provided. This builds the right brained picture connection for those talented right brained learners. Doing so also reinforces words in future reading that don't readily come to mind.

The Creative Writing pages are for your budding story teller to create a picture and story on any topic they wish. If they do not yet read, you could jot the story down for them. The parent sheets included after each lesson are for YOU to keep track of lessons learned, progress, notes on which activities were a hit…or not…and a place to jot down the ideas that you may have about future lessons. This is a great way to discover how your child learns and which methods you enjoy teaching most. It is also a great resource to document your spelling progress to your facilitator or other school authority.

Please do not stress over how much or how little your child accomplishes in this book. If they finish it in a year, that is great. If not; but they had fun learning some of the words, that is okay too. And not every child loves to colour. If they do; forcing it is a sure way to change that. The colouring pages included are in no way needed to build spelling skills. They are just a fun additive to colour while listening to the story. Same goes for the activity sheets: Feel free to leave them unfinished.

When you complete this book; take the momentum and run with it! Make up your own lists and invent new kinetic activities to spell with. Improved spelling is improved reading and writing.

That's it. Plain and simple. Learning can absolutely be fun. Try applying these lessons to your math and science and history studies. Implement movement in every lesson. Let your little one sit on a yoga ball and bounce. Add an active recess every 45 minutes. Let them squeeze a stress ball or toss a stuffy while studying. It may drive you crazy at first, but you will get used to it. Plus, if your see your child excelling at their academics, and enjoying it to boot; why not embrace that?

You can do this. You are a great person whose purchase of this book already proves that you are invested in finding the best possible education for your child. Willingness to try new methods makes you an amazing teacher. Finding a way to make your child succeed makes you a fantastic parent.

You got this.

If you need a little help, let us know. We are here for you.
brainbreakbooks@gmail.com.

Enjoy your learning together!

Bonus Activities

Here are some **more** ideas to keep your lessons active:

A. Write letters on index cards and place them across the room. Call out the word and have your child run to retrieve one letter at a time to spell the word. At first, you may want to call each letter until they see how they line up to spell the word.

B. Put some flour, sand or cornmeal in a cookie sheet and have your child spell their words by tracing them with their fingers.

C. Draw letters onto rocks and have the child toss them into the order of the word. Alternatively, chalk letters on a sidewalk or draw them on a paper randomly and have the child toss rocks to the letters to spell the words.

D. Write your spelling words onto paper airplanes. Shoot them into a laundry hamper or similar container. Any that do not land in the targeted area are read out loud letter by letter before taking another shot. They must be reshot until they land in as well.

E. Make up some soap paint and write the spelling words on the bathtub tiles at bath time. Or put bubbles on the wall and trace the words in them with fingers.

F. Put some finger paint in a ziploc bag and trace your words with a finger. Mess free painting!

G. Glue little magnets to letters you write on card stock squares. Practice spelling on the fridge! To keep it more active, include running for the letters from another location.

H. On a trampoline or bouncer ball, have the child recite the letters of each word and bouncing with each letter. Repeat each until several are learned. Have a dance party to celebrate!

I. Tape index cards with individual letters on the floor, spread out. Have the child run and stand on each letter as they say the spelling of the word out loud.

J. Hang strings from the roof, attaching an index card letter to each one. Call out a word and have your learner jump to touch each letter in order while saying the spelling out loud.

K. Chalk the letters on a large poster board randomly and give your child a fly swatter. Let them swat their spelling words, one letter at a time!

L. With a bucket of water and a paintbrush, send your speller outside to paint their words on the exterior house wall or sidewalk.

M. Place letters on floor and play "Spelling Twister"! Can your little keep contact with all the letters in a word?

N. Purchase or make your own letter dice and have your speller roll their spelling words out.

O. Have your student cut out paper strips and write letters on them. Using glue, let them turn their spelling list into paper chains.

P. Place magnetic alphabet tiles or lettered index cards on the floor so they are visible to your seated child. Have them use their feet to retrieve the letters in order to spell out their words.

Q. Using masking tape, mark out a maze on the floor with several turns. Call out the spelling word. Whenever your speller hits a turn, they must call out the letter needed before turning and continuing. If they make an error, they must go back to the previous turn. How many words will it take them to make it through the maze? (For more advanced learners, an error can send them back to the beginning).

Parent Planner

Lesson	Date to Complete	Notes
1		
2		
3		
4		
5		
6		
7		

Parent Planner Continued

8		
9		
10		
11		
12		
13		
14		
15		

LESSON 1

Sock Toss

All you need is a pair of socks balled up like a ball to toss back and forth for each letter you spell in lesson one's list. When you spell all of the words correctly go to the next lesson!

SPELLING LIST

1. will

2. too

3. ice

4. two

5. eat

6. who

7. you

8. but

9. ask

10. beg

Word Search

Can you find all the hidden spelling words in this table?

Words can go: ↑ ↓ → ↘ ↖

T	A	B	R	W	I	L	L
O	N	S	Y	U	Y	O	U
O	E	G	K	E	D	M	L
T	S	P	O	A	U	K	O
W	U	B	U	T	Q	H	S
O	V	H	B	C	W	L	I
R	B	E	G	I	Y	Z	C
P	A	J	O	L	X	V	E

BUT	BEG	WHO	YOU
EAT	TWO	TOO	
ICE	ASK	WILL	

LESSON 1 STORY

It was a hot summer day and a little pig sat to **eat** her **ice** cream. **Who** should come along but her friend; Kitty.

"**Will you** share with me? I **ask** because **you** have **two** scoops and I am so hot." Piggy said.

"I earned not one, **but** both scoops dancing at the fair."

"I cannot dance but I **beg** you to see my cartwheel!"

Kitty began turning cartwheels until Piggy fell over, giggling.

"Sit by me, Kitty, and enjoy some ice cream **too**!"

DOODLE
YOUR
DEFINITION

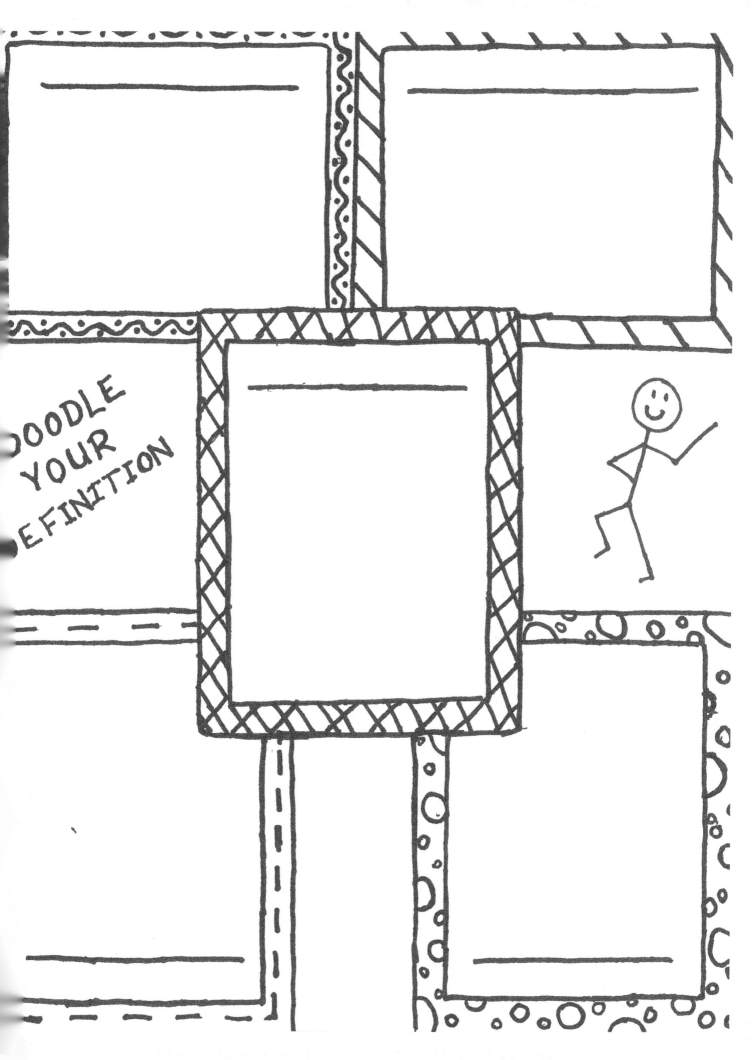

DOODLE YOUR DEFINITION

Definitions:

1. will - probability or choice

2. too - also, as well

3. ice - frozen liquid

4. two - more than one; less than three

5. eat - to consume (generally; food)

6. who - identifier of a person or individual

7. you - identifying a specific person

8. but - however

9. ask - to question

10. beg - to plead for

Creative Writing Page

Parent Sheet

Lesson: _____ Date: _____

Activity Used: _____ Fun? Y N

Word List: Mastered? (Circle if not)
1. will   ☐
2. too   ☐
3. ice   ☐
4. two   ☐
5. eat   ☐
6. who   ☐
7. you   ☐
8. but   ☐
9. ask   ☐
10. beg   ☐

Notes:

_____

_____

_____

_____

_____

How I am feeling today:

LESSON 2

Frog Hop

All you need for this activity is "YOU." The Parent is to say the word first, then have the child or children hop like a frog for each letter of the word. Then at the end, have the child say the word out loud, hop and say ribbit. Repeat this process with all the words in the list. You can add lily pads if you like and hop back one if a mistake is made. Continue until they get them all!

SPELLING LIST

1. few

2. one

3. ago

4. fly

5. won

6. pony

7. sea

8. does

9. war

10. our

Lesson 2

Can you draw a line matching the definition to the word?

1. more than one	A. ago
2. single	B. does
3. time past	C. war
4. propel above ground	D. sea
5. achieve	E. fly
6. small horse cousin	F. pony
7. ocean	G. one
8. present "do"	H. our
9. battle	I. few
10. belonging to us	J. won

Definitions:

1. few - a small group of

2. one - singular

3. ago - a time prior

4. fly - to propel in the air

5. won - to successfully achieve

6. pony - a smaller relative of the horse or to lead along

7. sea - ocean

8. does - present form of "do"

9. war - battle

10. our - belonging to us

LESSON 2 STORY

Long **ago**, a terrible **war** between the snails and the ladybugs caused shouting for weeks. **One** winged **pony**, tired of the noise, decided to **fly** over the **sea** in search of quiet. She landed on a beach and lay in the sun near a **few** rainbow starfish. Waking from her nap, she heard a soft voice.

"Excuse me," it called, "**Does** my dear pony have strong wings?"

"I do!" answered the winged pony, blinking her eyes at a lovely seahorse before her.

"**Our** kind can only swim," said the seahorse, "and I sneezed my tiara right into that tree!"

"I'll get it!" cried the pony, as she flew up and retrieved the crown from the branches, returning it to its' happy owner.

"You have **won** my friendship," smiled the seahorse, and she presented the pony with a beautiful necklace of pearls.

DOODLE YOUR DEFINITION

DOODLE YOUR DEFINITION

Lesson 2 Answers

Can you draw a line matching the definition to the word?

1. more than one I	A. ago
2. single G	B. does
3. time past A	C. war
4. propel above ground E	D. sea
5. achieve J	E. fly
6. small horse cousin F	F. pony
7. ocean D	G. one
8. present "do" B	H. our
9. battle C	I. few
10. belonging to us H	J. won

Creative Writing Page

Parent Sheet

Lesson: _____ Date: _____

Activity Used: _____ Fun? Y N

Word List: **Mastered? (Circle if not)**

1. few   ☐
2. one   ☐
3. ago   ☐
4. fly   ☐
5. won   ☐
6. pony   ☐
7. sea   ☐
8. does   ☐
9. war   ☐
10. our   ☐

Notes:

_____

_____

_____

_____

How I am feeling today:

LESSON 3

Hand Clap

All you need for this activity is "YOU." Have the child first say the word out loud. Then, have the child clap out each letter of the word. Once they have completed saying each letter of the word, have them say the word out loud.

SPELLING LIST

1. why

2. tall

3. ears

4. pull

5. said

6. eyes

7. again

8. don't

9. ugly

10. every

Alphabetize

Your spelling list is split into two groups of 5. Can you list each in alphabetical order?

List A:	List B:
again	every
said	pull
eyes	why
ugly	ear
tall	don't

Definitions:

1. why - to question about reasons for things occurring

2. tall - opposite of short

3. ears - fleshy appendages that allow for hearing

4. pull - opposite of push

5. said - spoke in the past

6. eyes - facial features responsible for sight

7. again - repeated

8. don't - abbreviated form of "do not"

9. ugly - unattractive, opposite of beautiful

10. every - each

LESSON 3 STORY

Every morning, the **ears** sat **tall**, gazing longingly at the bright green **eyes**.

"Why must we be so **ugly** and you so shining?" Ears asked.

"**Don't** say that," **said** Eyes, "**Why** long for sight when you bring us music?"

Still, each day, when Hands decided to **pull** out a sparkling pair of earrings and attach them to Ears. They were dazzling!

Eyes grinned and Ears never felt less than pretty ever **again**.

DOODLE
YOUR
DEFINITION

DOODLE
YOUR
DEFINITION

Alphabetize Answers

Your spelling list is split into two groups of 5. Can you list each in alphabetical order?

List A:

again

said

eyes

ugly

tall

List B:

every

pull

why

ear

don't

again	don't
eyes	ear
said	every
tall	pull
ugly	why

Creative Writing Page

Parent Sheet

Lesson: _____ Date: _____

Activity Used: _____ Fun? Y N

Word List:	Mastered? (Circle if not)
1. why	☐
2. tall	☐
3. ears	☐
4. pull	☐
5. said	☐
6. eyes	☐
7. again	☐
8. don't	☐
9. ugly	☐
10. every	☐

Notes:

_____

_____

_____

_____

How I am feeling today:

LESSON 4

Jumping Jacks

For this activity, you can have your child do a jumping jack for each letter of the word or they can just do the jumping jacks and say the word out loud. You may alternate with push ups, sit ups, etc.

SPELLING LIST

1. back

2. when

3. they

4. each

5. goes

6. know

7. then

8. cube

9. nice

10. rage

MISSING LETTERS

Fill in the missing letters in each word.

back   when   they   rage

each   goes   know   nice

then   cube

__ o e s   w __ e __

n __ c __   __ n o __

t h __ __   r __ __ e

__ __ e y   b a __ __

e __ c __   c __ b __

Definitions:

1. back - the opposite of front or forward

2. when - place in time

3. they - grouping of individuals

4. each - individual identifier

5. goes - present tense of "go"

6. know - learned, to have information of

7. then - a future time

8. cube - a three dimensional square

9. nice - pleasant

10. rage - extreme anger

LESSON 4 STORY

Way **back when**, boys often spent long afternoons fishing in creeks. **Each** used a long stick as a rod and baited it with a worm or a **cube** of bread.

On **nice** days of hot sunshine, you **know** how it goes; cool water invites splashing.

One boy would splash another and soon **they** all would be swimming and laughing in the cold water. Hours would slip by as clouds rolled in.

Then a storm would **rage** and all the boys would race home for hot cocoa.

DOODLE YOUR DEFINITION

DOODLE YOUR DEFINITION

MISSING LETTERS ANSWER

Fill in the missing letters in each word.

back	when	they	rage
each	goes	know	nice
then	cube		

_G_ o e s   w _H_ e _N_

n _I_ c _E_   _K_ n o _W_

t h _E_ _N_   r _A_ _G_ e

_T_ _H_ e y   b a _C_ _K_

e _A_ c _H_   c _U_ b _E_

Creative Writing Page

Parent Sheet

Lesson: _____ Date: _____

Activity Used: _____ Fun? Y N

Word List: Mastered? (Circle if not)
1. back   ☐
2. when   ☐
3. they   ☐
4. each   ☐
5. goes   ☐
6. know   ☐
7. then   ☐
8. cube   ☐
9. nice   ☐
10. rage   ☐

Notes:

_____

_____

_____

_____

How I am feeling today:

LESSON 5

Let's Run

All you need for this activity is sneakers and scissors. Cut out the Word Wall list in the book. Place the words in different places outside or in your home. Parents call out the words and have the child run to find the word that you say. Once the child finds the word, have them touch the word and say it out loud. For extra fun; add a timer!

This is also a great activity to do with a group.

SPELLING LIST

1. used

2. sure

3. calm

4. only

5. hurt

6. come

7. okay

8. high

9. road

10. mold

sure

calm

only

okay

come

hurt

used

mold

road

Definitions:

1. used - not new, to have endured use of

2. sure - agreement, confidence in

3. calm - to be in a gentle state of mind

4. only - singular

5. hurt - to be in pain or to cause pain

6. come - to move toward something

7. okay - affirming health, to agree

8. high - opposite of low

9. road - a pathway

10. mold - a fungus

LESSON 5 STORY

"**Come** on, Brigette!" Atticus called from **high** up the tree.

"I can see the **road** from up here," she replied, running her hand over a patch of green on the bark. "Is this tree **mold**?"

"No," her brother pulled her up to his level. "It's moss."

"I could **sure** get **used** to this," Brigette smiled.

"Let's go higher!"

Atticus caught her arm, shaking his head and pointing up.

"Stay **calm** and they won't **hurt** you."

Brigette gazed up at the beehive buzzing with activity above their heads.

"**Only** you would choose to climb a honey tree," whispered Brigette.

Atticus grinned. "We're **okay**…but let's go swing on the swing set instead."

DOODLE YOUR DEFINITION

DOODLE
YOUR
DEFINITION

Creative Writing Page

Parent Sheet

Lesson: _____ Date: _____

Activity Used: _____ Fun? Y N

Word List:	Mastered? (Circle if not)
1. used	☐
2. sure	☐
3. calm	☐
4. only	☐
5. hurt	☐
6. come	☐
7. okay	☐
8. high	☐
9. road	☐
10. mold	☐

Notes:

_____

_____

_____

_____

How I am feeling today: 😃 😜 😔 😠 😳 😍 🧐 😖

Parent Check Up

You are 1/3 done!

In the last 5 lessons, which words or activities did your child enjoy the most? Have your student write or draw their answer here and discuss.

LESSON 6

Singing

Now it is time to exercise those lungs. It is time to sing! You can choose any tune or music you like. You don't even have to use music. For this activity, just spell your words out with song. While you are singing, make it a full body experience. Clap your hands, move from side to side, or dance. Have Fun!!!

SPELLING LIST

1. boat

2. wait

3. stair

4. hour

5. scary

6. white

7. race

8. oil

9. head

10. sorry

LESSON 6 STORY

"**Sorry** I'm late," Caterpillar hurried down the **stair** and into the **boat**."

"You know I would **wait** for you," smiled the little white **mouse**, "but the **hour** is late and we must hurry to the party."

The boat set off down the canal, bobbing in the sparkling water.

"Be careful of that **oil** tug," Caterpillar pointed out, setting Mouse to the sail to steer around it.

Suddenly, a current caught hold of the little boat and sucked it down into a drain tunnel.

"Keep your **head** down!" cried Mouse as the boat began to **race** and spin out of control.

Peeking from between their fingers, the two animals saw their craft emerge back into the sunshiny canal and their friends were waving merrily from the dock.

"Well," smiled Caterpillar, "It was **scary**, but what a short cut!"

DOODLE
YOUR
DEFINITION

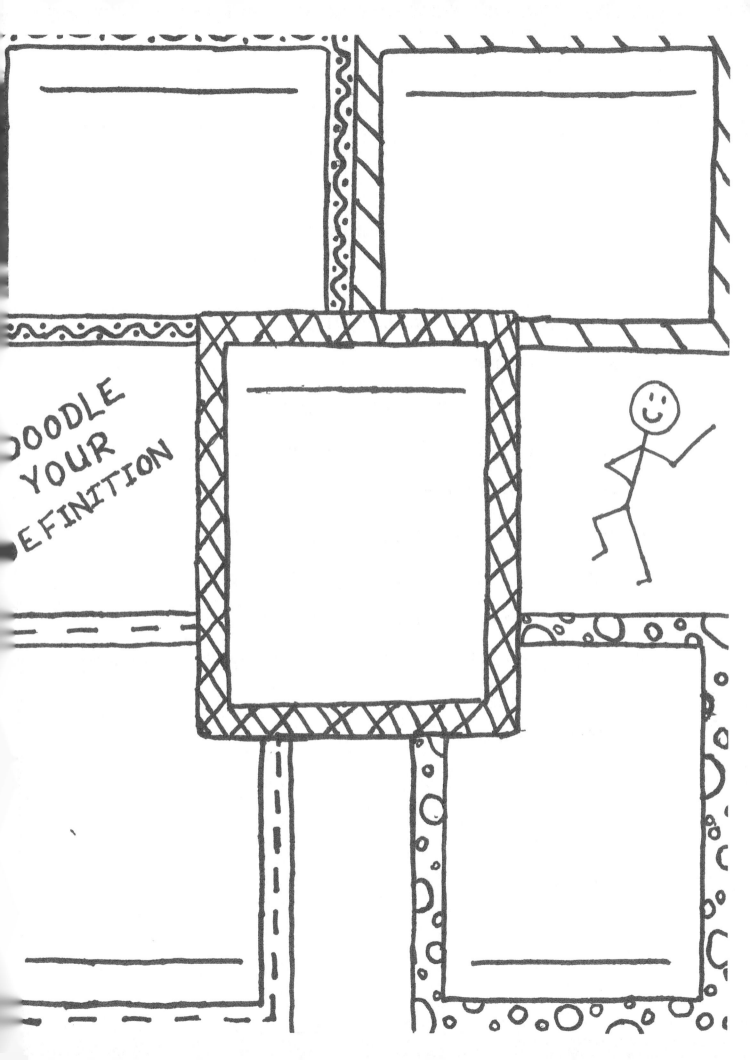

DOODLE YOUR DEFINITION

Definitions:

1. boat - a vessel for water transport

2. wait - to pause

3. stair - steps to reach another level

4. hour - a 60 minute time increment

5. scary - situation causing fear

6. white - a colour representing blankness

7. race - to compete or a cultural identification

8. oil - a liquid extract causing slickness

9. head - the body part on the neck housing a skull and brain, to lead

10. sorry - apology

Creative Writing Page

Lesson 6
Complete the crossword below.

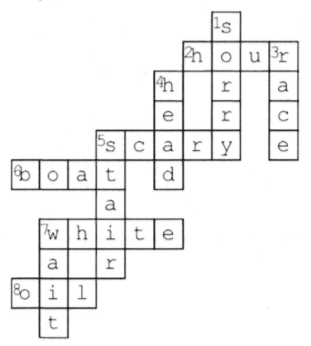

Parent Sheet

Lesson: _____ Date: _____

Activity Used: _____ Fun? Y N

Word List: Mastered? (Circle if not)
1. boat   ☐
2. wait   ☐
3. stair   ☐
4. hour   ☐
5. scary   ☐
6. white   ☐
7. race   ☐
8. oil   ☐
9. head   ☐
10. sorry   ☐

Notes:

_____

_____

_____

_____

How I am feeling today: 😀 🤪 😔 😡 😳 😍 🧐 😖

Lesson 6

Complete the crossword below.

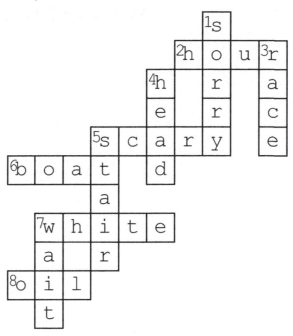

Across

2. 60 minutes (**ho ur**)
5. frightening (**scary**)
6. a floating vessel (**bo at**)
7. pure, blank colour (**whit e**)
8. a lubricating fluid (**o il**)

Down

1. to apologize (**so rry**)
3. to compete with, to speed (**race**)
4. to lead, or the skull containing the brain (**he ad**)
5. a step up or down to another level (**st air**)
7. to pause or hesitate (**wait**)

LESSON 7

Squats

All you need to do in this activity is to say the words out loud then squat for each letter. Once the child is finish spelling the word out with squats have the child stand straight and say the word out loud again. Continue this with the complete list.

SPELLING LIST

1. many

2. once

3. bear

4. place

5. very

6. hair

7. blue

8. long

9. home

10. made

Lesson 7 Word Scramble

many	made	very
once	hair	home
bear	blue	long
	place	

Can you unscramble the following words from your spelling list?

arbe _____

glon _____

lube _____

nyma _____

deam _____

irha _____

cone _____

meoh _____

revy _____

clape _____

Definitions:

1. many - several

2. once - one time

3. bear - a large forest dwelling animal

4. place - location

5. very - extremely

6. hair - fine growth from top of head or from skin

7. blue - colour of a sunny sky

8. long - opposite of short

9. home - dwelling

10. made - to create

LESSON 7 STORY

Once upon a time, there was a **very** sweet **bear** with **long, blue hair**.

It was only fall but already the winter cold was creeping in. Bear took one final forest walk before making her **home** in her cave until spring. **Many** forest creatures were shivering, already too cold in the worsening weather.

Bear thought of her big, lonely cave, and of all the dear friends she had **made**, who were freezing outside.

"Attention, friends!" Bear said, "If you need a **place** to sleep winter away, I welcome you to my home."

Hopping, tip toeing and creeping, creatures came into the cozy cave.

When winter struck that night, Bear was cuddled up warmly with her friends nestled against her, her long blue hair snuggled around them all.

DOODLE
YOUR
DEFINITION

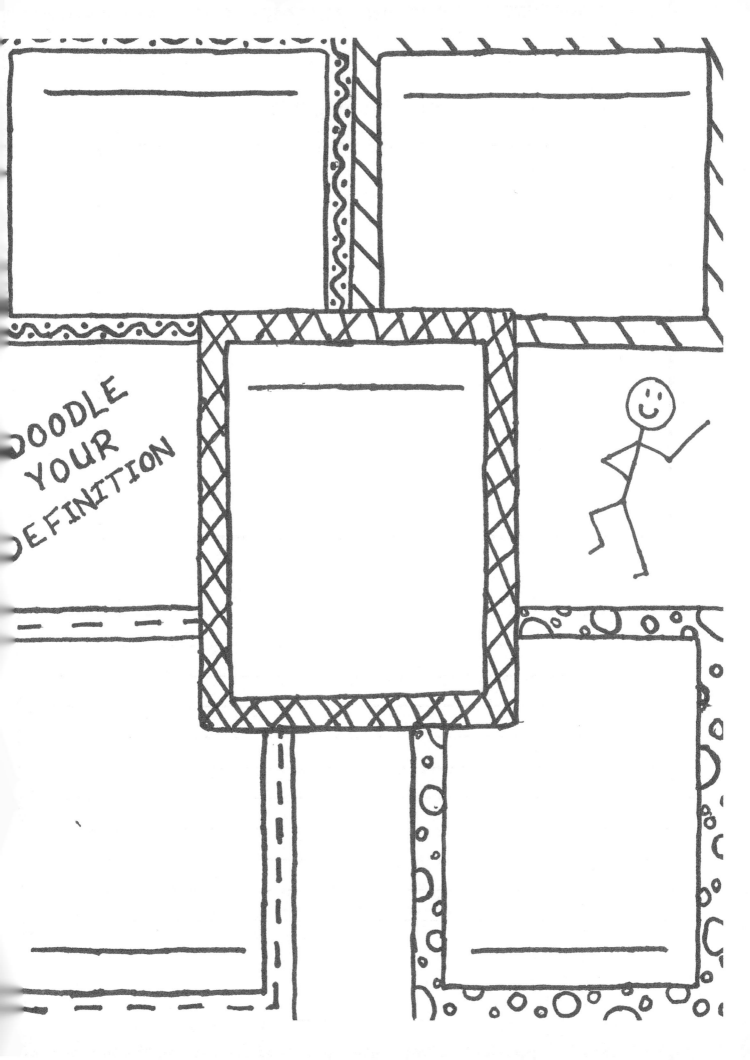

DOODLE YOUR DEFINITION

Creative Writing Page

_____
_____
_____
_____
_____
_____
_____
_____
_____
_____
_____

Parent Sheet

Lesson: _____ Date: _____

Activity Used: _____ Fun? Y N

Word List: Mastered? (Circle if not)

1. many   ☐
2. once   ☐
3. bear   ☐
4. place   ☐
5. very   ☐
6. hair   ☐
7. blue   ☐
8. long   ☐
9. home   ☐
10. made   ☐

Notes:

_____

_____

_____

_____

How I am feeling today:

LESSON 8

Word Hunt

For this activity the child should roam around the house and look for the words in this spelling list in the home. They can look at books, boxes, magazines, games, etc. Just look for the words everywhere. You can time it if you like.

SPELLING LIST

1. please

2. music

3. wonder

4. dollar

5. threw

6. money

7. blood

8. huge

9. cloud

10. whose

LESSON 8 ACTIVITY

Can you use each word in a sentence? Have fun with it!

1. please - _____

   _____

   _____

2. music - _____

   _____

   _____

3. wonder - _____

   _____

   _____

4. dollar - _____

   _____

   _____

5. threw - _____

   _____

   _____

6. money - _____

_____

_____

7. blood - _____

_____

_____

8. huge - _____

_____

_____

9. cloud - _____

_____

_____

10. whose - _____

_____

_____

Definitions:

1. please - to make happy, to request

2. music - melody

3. wonder - question, be curious about

4. dollar - an increment of money, one hundred cents

5. threw - to have tossed

6. money - currency

7. blood - life giving fluid present inside body

8. huge - large

9. cloud - a floating cluster of moisture

10. whose - questioning of possession

LESSON 8 STORY

"May I **please** buy this **blood** orange? I have a **dollar** here."

Cheridynn gave the lady the **money** and walked past the market stalls. She found a **huge** stone shadowing a charming wishing well. She sat to eat her orange and watch the **clouds** drift past.

"I **wonder** what you'll wish for," Tazhae, Cheridynns' best friend sat beside her and held out a coin.

"I didn't hear you coming," Cher smiled.

"The market **music** is pretty loud," Tazhae replied. "Now, **whose** heart will you wish for in this magic well?"

Cheridynn rolled her eyes, paused, then **threw** the coin into the wells' depths. There was a falling tinkling, a faint splash, then a tiny meow.

The startled girls glanced at each other, then quickly pulled up the bucket, revealing a tiny spotted kitten.

"This well *is* magic," Cher declared, "My wish came true!"

DOODLE YOUR DEFINITION

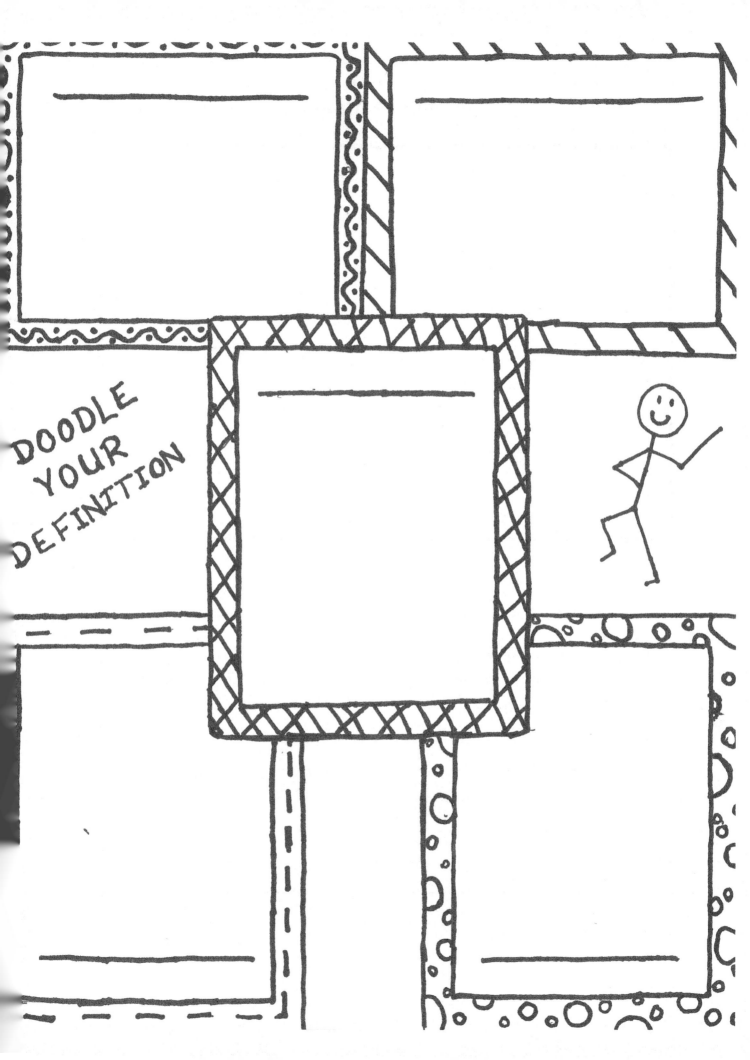

DOODLE YOUR DEFINITION

Creative Writing Page

Parent Sheet

Lesson: _____ Date: _____

Activity Used: _____ Fun? Y N

Word List: Mastered? (Circle if not)
1. please   ☐
2. music   ☐
3. wonder   ☐
4. dollar   ☐
5. threw   ☐
6. money   ☐
7. blood   ☐
8. huge   ☐
9. cloud   ☐
10. whose   ☐
Notes:

_____

_____

_____

_____

How I am feeling today: 😃 🤪 😔 😡 😳 😍 🧐 😖

LESSON 9

Let's Create

For this activity you are going to use your creative side. All you do is make up a song and dance using your spelling list. Or try a poem and a skit.

Your imagination will lead the way!

SPELLING LIST

1. gone
2. ninth
3. would
4. coming
5. poison
6. ready
7. police
8. animal
9. actual
10. noise

LESSON 9 ACTIVITY

Using two words at once, can you mix the letters together to form other words? An example is given for you.

would, coming

___cold___   ___mold___   ___wing___

poison, animal

_____   _____   _____

actual, ninth

_____   _____   _____

ready, police

_____   _____   _____

gone, noise

_____   _____   _____

LESSON 9 STORY

"This is the **ninth** street we have checked," Atticus sighed, "We may never find my dog. I knew he was afraid of **noise**. I should have been **ready** for the fireworks."

"Don't worry," Isaiah reassured him, "I am more thorough than a **police** detective." He bent down at a hedge. "These branches are bent. A person **would** never crawl through brush this thick. But an **animal** might."

"Gandalf!" Atticus called, holding out some chocolate.

"Not that!" Isaiah pushed away the chocolate bar. "Chocolate will **poison** a dog, I brought cheese instead."

The two boys crouched over some paw prints.

"These are far apart," Isaiah observed, "Gandalf was running."

"Wow!" Atticus smiled, "You are an **actual** tracker."

The tracks disappeared into grass. Isaiah paused.

"If I was a dog, where would I have **gone**?" He breathed in deeply, then raced up the alley, stopping to peer into a fenced yard, where a barbecue was in full swing.

"Gandalf!" Atticus called.

When he saw the boys **coming**, Gandalf started wagging his tail, a hamburger in his mouth.

"He has good taste!" laughed Isaiah.

Definitions:

1. gone - to have disappeared

2. ninth - the item in a line; one more than eight

3. would - will do

4. coming - in motion towards something

5. poison - contaminate causing illness

6. ready - prepared

7. police - military type law enforcement

8. animal - non-human creature

9. actual - real

10. noise - sound

Creative Writing Page

DOODLE YOUR DEFINITION

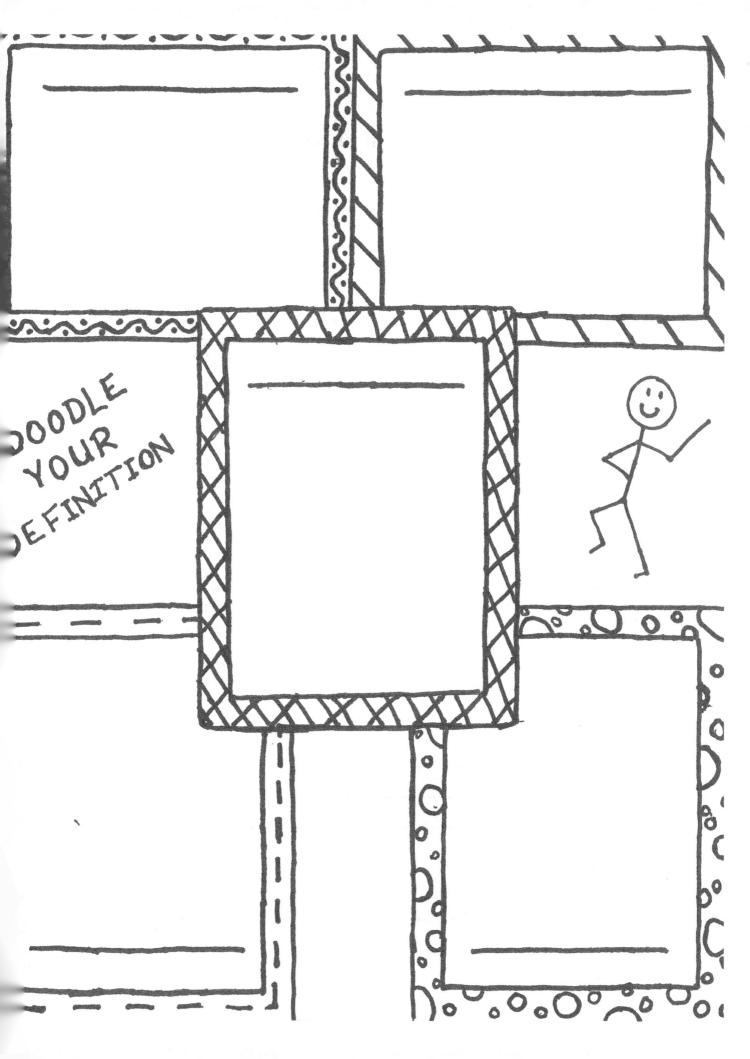

DOODLE YOUR DEFINITION

Parent Sheet

Lesson: _____ Date: _____

Activity Used: _____ Fun? Y N

Word List: Mastered? (Circle if not)

1. gone   ☐
2. ninth   ☐
3. would   ☐
4. coming   ☐
5. poison   ☐
6. ready   ☐
7. police   ☐
8. animal   ☐
9. actual   ☐
10. noise   ☐

Notes:

_____

_____

_____

_____

How I am feeling today:

LESSON 10

Jump Rope

Let's pull out that jump rope and use it to spell our words. * If you do not have a jump rope just jump in place. All you do for this activity is jump and say your words while jumping.

SPELLING LIST

1. their

2. watch

3. fairy

4. about

5. right

6. daily

7. where

8. large

9. night

10. autumn

LESSON 10 ACTIVITY

Repetition helps us learn. Write each spelling word 3 times, but have fun with it! Use fun colours or squiggly lines; even cursive!

their

——————————   ——————————   ——————————

watch

——————————   ——————————   ——————————

fairy

——————————   ——————————   ——————————

about

——————————   ——————————   ——————————

right

——————————   ——————————   ——————————

daily

——————————   ——————————   ——————————

where

——————————   ——————————   ——————————

large

——————————   ——————————   ——————————

night

——————————   ——————————   ——————————

autumn

——————————   ——————————   ——————————

Definitions:

1. their - belonging to them

2. watch - observe

3. fairy - a mythical creature

4. about - reasonably close to

5. right - opposite of left. correct

6. daily - every day

7. where - a location

8. large - big

9. night - opposite of day

10. autumn - fall season

LESSON 10 STORY

It was just **about their** bedtime for the Androschuk family. Éowynn couldn't find her little sister. She headed into the **autumn** air, knowing **right where** Brigette spent as many hours as she could **daily**. Sure enough, Brigette was settled on a bed of moss, staring at the painted leaves dancing in the waterfall.

"Crouch down!" whispered Brigette, "They won't come around **large** people. You must be tiny."

"They?" Éowynn ducked into the crackling leaves.

"I want to see a **fairy** dance."

Éowynn opened her mouth to object but changed her mind. The girls settled in to **watch** the sparkling water, to hear the melody of birds in the crisp air and the gurgling splashes of the escaping creek.

They cuddled in silence, seeing squirrels and rabbits scurrying through the crunchy leaves.

At last, **night** had come and the sisters crept home hand in hand under the twinkling stars. They might not have seen a fairy, but were filled to the brim with the magic every forest holds.

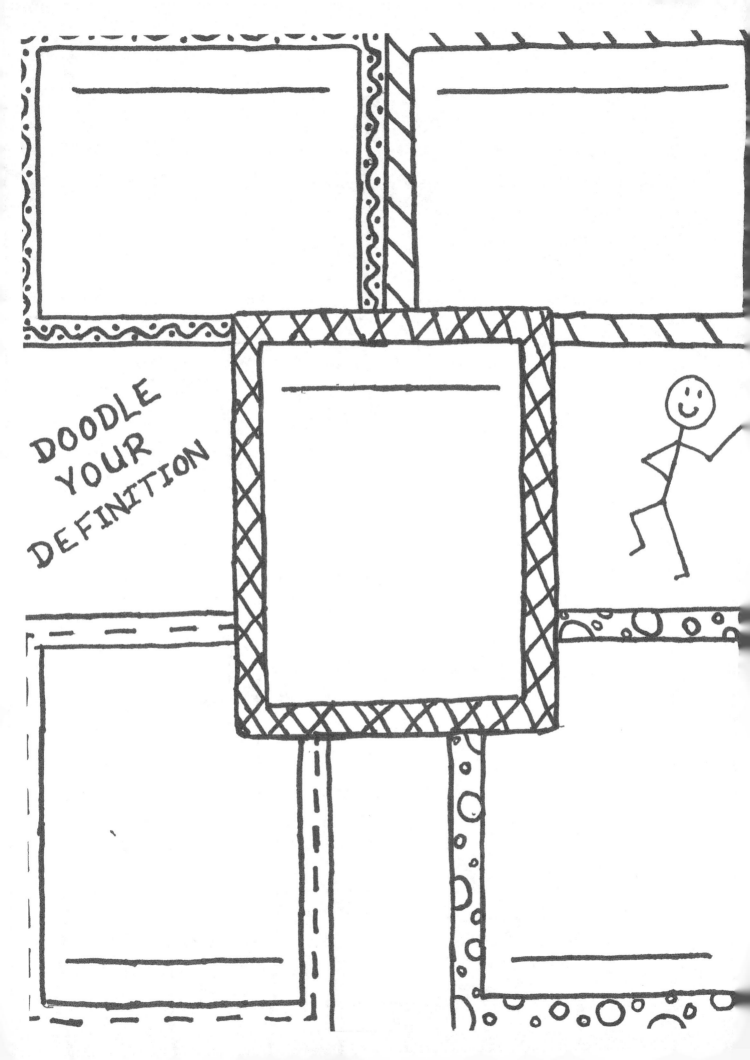

DOODLE
YOUR
DEFINITION

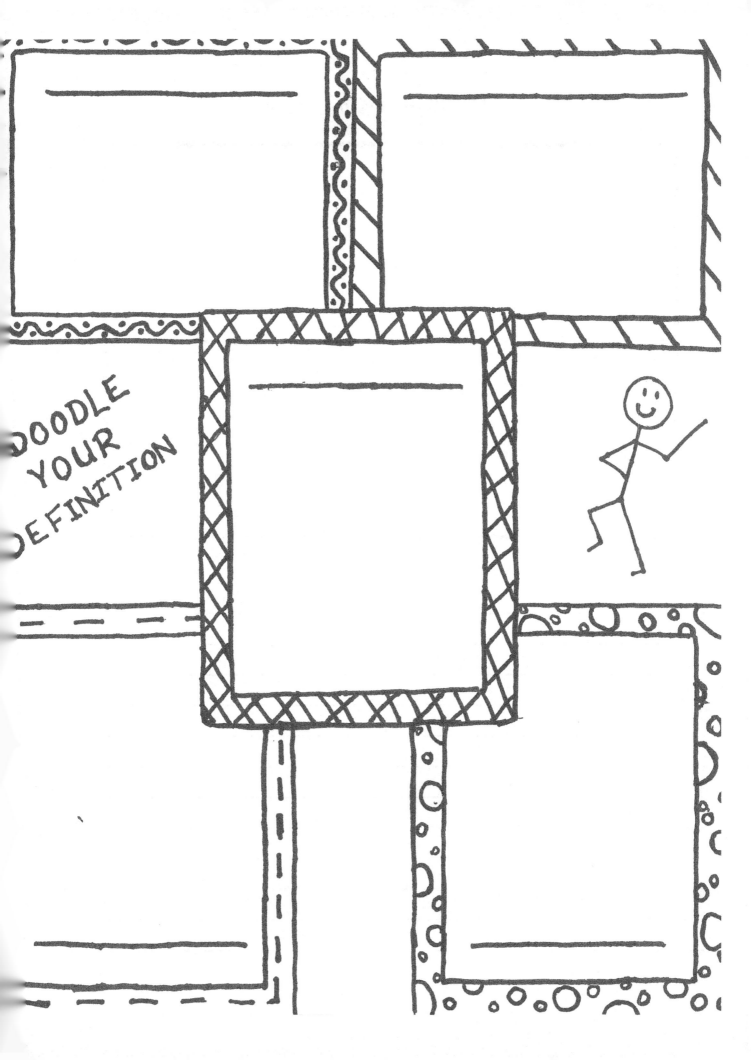

DOODLE YOUR DEFINITION

Creative Writing Page

_____
_____
_____
_____
_____
_____
_____
_____
_____
_____
_____

Parent Sheet

Lesson: _____ Date: _____

Activity Used: _____ Fun? Y N

Word List: Mastered? (Circle if not)
1. their   ☐
2. watch   ☐
3. fairy   ☐
4. about   ☐
5. right   ☐
6. daily   ☐
7. where   ☐
8. large   ☐
9. night   ☐
10. autumn   ☐

Notes:

_____

_____

_____

_____

How I am feeling today: 😀 😜 😔 😠 😳 😍 🧐 😣

Parent Check Up

You are 2/3 done!

In the last 5 lessons, which words or activities did your child enjoy the most? Have your student write or draw their answer here and discuss.

LESSON 11

Game Show

For this activity the Parent or one of your children will call out a word from the list. Use a buzzer or bell to play. The child that buzzes in first, and spells the word out loud, correctly; wins.

SPELLING LIST

1. which
2. sleepy
3. heard
4. great
5. while
6. fourth
7. didn't
8. caught
9. pretty
10. laugh(ed)

LESSON 11 STORY

"**Which** of you last saw Hagrid?" the boy asked the long row of children in beds.

"I **didn't** see him at all this evening," one child answered from the first bed.

The boy went to the second bed.

"Have you seen him?"

"Not in a long **while**," a **sleepy** voice replied.

"Did you put Hagrid outside?" he asked the child in the third bed.

"No," yawned the little one kicking off slippers, "I last saw him before supper when he **caught** a mouse in the pantry. He is a **great** mouser."

"I know," sighed the boy, "but I get **pretty** worried when he disappears like this."

As he approached the **fourth** bed, the boy froze. The beds' occupant was fast asleep, but beneath the blankets, a gentle purr could be **heard**. A slight tug on the blankets revealed the tiny cat curled up, his tail wrapped right around his pink nose. The boy **laughed**.

"No wonder she's asleep… You do make the best teddy bear, Hagrid!"

Definitions:

1. which - specifying one or another

2. sleepy - tired

3. heard - to hear something in the past

4. great - big, wonderful

5. while - a time period, during

6. fourth - the number four item in a row

7. didn't - abbreviation of "did not"

8. caught - to procure something

9. pretty - beautiful

10. laugh(ed) - giggle openmouthed

Fit each of the words below into a word shape puzzle.

which   sleepy   heard   great   while

fourth   didn't   caught   pretty   laughed

DOODLE
YOUR
DEFINITION

DOODLE YOUR DEFINITION

Creative Writing Page

Parent Sheet

Lesson: _____ Date: _____

Activity Used: _____ Fun? Y N

Word List: Mastered? (Circle if not)
1. which   ☐
2. sleepy   ☐
3. heard   ☐
4. great   ☐
5. while   ☐
6. fourth   ☐
7. didn't   ☐
8. caught   ☐
9. pretty   ☐
10. laugh(ed)   ☐

Notes:

_____

_____

_____

_____

How I am feeling today:

Answers

Fit each of the words below into a word shape puzzle.

which   sleepy   heard   great   while

fourth   didn't   caught   pretty   laughed

laughed   sleepy

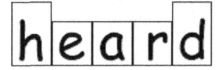

heard   didn t

caught   great

which   pretty

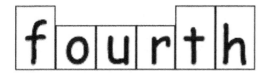

fourth   while

LESSON 12

Letters

For this activity we will be using magnet letters, scrabble letters, foam letters or make your own letters with index cards. Mix the letters up on a table and then give the child a word from the list to spell. *Bonus: have the child make up a sentence using the word once they spell the word out correctly.

SPELLING LIST

1. magical

2. since

3. half

4. awful

5. country

6. fence

7. hospital

8. knife

9. flour

10. flower

Lesson 12

Dot to Dot! Feel free to draw in details once the image is drawn.
What creature is it?

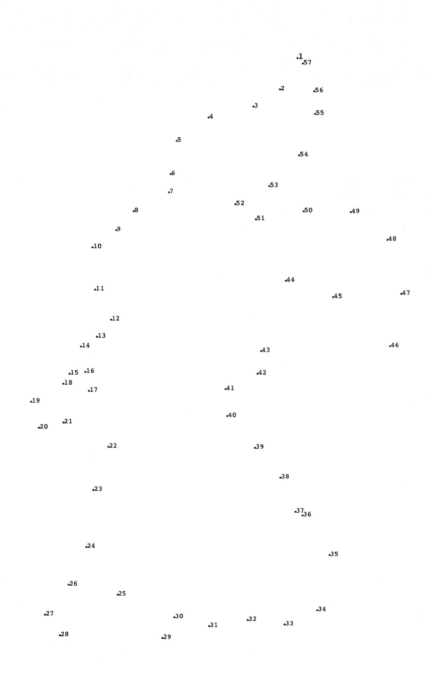

Definitions:

1. magical - having a quality of magic about it

2. since - after a time in the past

3. half - a portion of an item, equal to one part of two

4. awful - terrible

5. country - a self governed area made up of smaller territories

6. fence - a man made obstruction walling an area

7. hospital - a place to recieve medical attention

8. knife - a sharp weapon

9. flour - a powdery form of ground grains used for breads

10. flower - a plant possessing blossoms

LESSON 12 STORY

Big Bunny hopped carefully past the **fence** up to Little Bunnys' lemonade stand.

"Where are you off to?" asked Little Bunny, "You are covered in **flour**!" He giggled.

"Well," said Big Bunny, wiping her paws on her apron, "I was trying to bake cookies today, but ever **since** that scorching sun came out, I have a headache that cuts like a **knife**. She sighed, smoothing her whiskers, "Now I must hop across **country** to the animal **hospital**."

"You must feel **awful**!" lamented Little Bunny. "Come sit here in the shade. I will give you **half** a glass for free."

Big Bunny sipped the lemonade, letting the fragrant **flowers** tickle her nose as she cooled off in the shade. Minutes later, she pulled a coin from her apron.

"Your biggest glass, please, Little Bunny! This lemonade is **magical**; my headache is gone!"

Little Bunny brought a tall glass over.

"Thank you." Big Bunny winked at him, "Now I will head home and when you come to collect your glass, I will share my magical cookies!"

DOODLE YOUR DEFINITION

DOODLE YOUR DEFINITION

Lesson 12 Answer

Creative Writing Page

Parent Sheet

Lesson: _____ Date: _____

Activity Used: _____ Fun? Y N

Word List: Mastered? (Circle if not)

1. magical   ☐
2. since   ☐
3. half   ☐
4. awful   ☐
5. country   ☐
6. fence   ☐
7. hospital   ☐
8. knife   ☐
9. flour   ☐
10. flower   ☐

Notes:

_____

_____

_____

_____

How I am feeling today: 😀 🤪 😔 😠 😳 😍 🧐 😖

LESSON 13

Stomping

Let's get ready to stomp our words out. Just stomp as you call each letter of the spelling words out loud. Be creative and have fun spelling. Alternatively, instead of stomping, you can clap, kick, punch a pillow…or pat different parts of your body for each letter.

SPELLING LIST

1. minutes

2. science

3. field

4. round

5. always

6. whole

7. almost

8. wreck

9. muscle

10. weather

LESSON 13 STORY

"Every **muscle** in my legs ache," Éowynn groaned. "I have **almost** been over this **whole field** a hundred times."

Cheridynn laughed.

"I have been watching you. What are you looking for?"

Éowynn sat down, tucking her magnifying glass in her pocket.

"You know…**science**. Something to base a project on. Cool bugs, plants, rocks…anything. Instead, I just keep going **round** and round waiting for something to catch my attention."

"What about studying **weather**? I heard thunder a few **minutes** ago."

Right then, the sky darkened as the sun slid behind dark clouds.

"Run for it!"

The two sisters screamed, startled by a flash of lightning and a booming crack of thunder. They splashed through mud, **wrecking** their pretty sundresses as rain pelted them mercilessly.

Slamming the door behind them, the girls stood in the mudroom, rain streaming from their clothes.

"I think I'll study weather," Éowynn gasped, "Storms **always** have a way of grabbing my attention!"

Lesson 13 Activity

Choose any 2 words from your spelling list and see how many words you can make from them. Good luck!

_____

_____   _____

_____   _____

_____   _____

_____   _____

_____

_____   _____

_____   _____

_____   _____

_____   _____

Definitions:

1. minutes - time increments, each minute consisting of 60 seconds

2. science - the study of living and non-living things

3. field - an area of land

4. round - circular

5. always - consistently

6. whole - all, entire

7. almost - very close to

8. wreck - ruin

9. muscle - tissue inside the body giving strength, to force

10. weather - all goings on of natural forces in the sky

DOODLE
YOUR
DEFINITION

DOODLE YOUR DEFINITION

Creative Writing Page

Parent Sheet

Lesson: _____ Date: _____

Activity Used: _____ Fun? Y N

Word List:	Mastered? (Circle if not)
1. minutes	☐
2. science	☐
3. field	☐
4. round	☐
5. always	☐
6. whole	☐
7. almost	☐
8. wreck	☐
9. muscle	☐
10. weather	☐

Notes:

_____

_____

_____

_____

How I am feeling today: 😀 🤪 😔 😡 😳 😍 🧐 😖

LESSON 14

Hopscotch

All you do in this activity is make a hopscotch board and in the squares of the board, put the first letter of each word in this spelling list. Then, have the child, or children, throw a rock onto the hopscotch board. Whatever letter the rock lands on, the child will spell the word that goes with that letter. Repeat the process until you have spelled all your words in the spelling list.

SPELLING LIST

1. sugar

2. juicy

3. heart

4. giant

5. tired

6. buying

7. wives

8. color/colour

9. ghost

10. usually

Lesson 14 Activity

Get out the scissors and glue!

Here are some letter flashcards to spell out your whole spelling list and paste them to a piece of paper.

Happy gluing!

a	a	a	a	b
c	c	d	e	e
e	g	g	g	g
h	h	i	i	i
i	i	j	l	l
l	n	n	o	o

o	r	r	r	r
s	s	s	s	t
t	t	t	u	u
u	u	u	u	v
w				

Definitions:

1. sugar - a sweet extract

2. juicy - moist

3. heart - the organ responsible for pumping blood

4. giant - a large item or creature

5. tired - sleepy

6. buying - purchasing

7. wives - several female spouses

8. color/colour - shade of

9. ghost - an apparition

10. usually - generally

LESSON 14 STORY

Isaiah was just about to bite into a **juicy** mango when his sister, Tazhae, walked in.

"Are you done your bible study?" she asked, "I saw you at the store **buying** a bunch of **sugar** candies. That **usually** means you are done working."

"No," Isaiah admitted, "my **heart** isn't in it today. Ancient Israel is mostly sand and long walks. I am **tired** of reading about boring stuff."

"Boring?" Tazhae was surprised. "A boy killing a **giant**" A talking donkey? Isaiah, as a man then, you would already have been buying land, working a trade, supporting your **wives**…"

"Wives!" Isaiah blanched.

Tazhae laughed. "Brother, you're the **colour** of a **ghost**!"

Creative Writing Page

_____

_____

_____

_____

_____

_____

_____

_____

_____

_____

Parent Sheet

Lesson: _____ Date: _____

Activity Used: _____ Fun? Y N

Word List: Mastered? (Circle if not)
1. sugar   ☐
2. juicy   ☐
3. heart   ☐
4. giant   ☐
5. tired   ☐
6. buying   ☐
7. wives   ☐
8. color/colour   ☐
9. ghost   ☐
10. usually   ☐
Notes:

_____

_____

_____

_____

How I am feeling today: 😃 🤪 😔 😡 😳 😍 🧐 😖

DOODLE YOUR DEFINITION

DOODLE YOUR DEFINITION

LESSON 15

Playdough

For this activity you will need playdough, or anything that will allow you to create letters with. Have the child spell out the word list with playdough. You can also carve the words into the dough with a toothpick. *Bonus; you can let the childs' playdough words dry in the sun to make their own Word Art Museum. They can paint the words after they dry.

SPELLING LIST

1. chicken

2. clothes

3. potato

4. rough

5. monkey

6. babies

7. pickle

8. nothing

9. answer

10. dinosaur

LESSON 15 ACTIVITY

Mirror Image

Have you ever tried to write messages that you can read in a mirror? Use your spelling list to give it a try!

1. chicken

2. clothes

3. potato

4. rough

5. monkey

6. babies

7. pickle

8. nothing

9. answer

10. dinosaur

LESSON 15 STORY

"Isaiah is the **monkey** in the middle!" Éowynn called.

"Let's switch to **chicken** fights," suggested Tazhae.

"Those get too **rough**." Cheridynn noted, "How about relay races instead?"

"I don't want to get my **clothes** dirty." said Brigette.

Atticus had an idea.

"We can do **potato** sack races!"

"Or **pickle** ball," **answered** Brigette.

"Let's invent our own game," said Isaiah, authoritatively. "I'll be the Daddy **dinosaur**. You guys be the dinosaur **babies**. Hide. I'll find you and chase you back to the nest here. Any objections?"

With big grins, everyone raced off to hide. Until dusk, the yard was filled with the shrieks and laughter of joyous children having **nothing** but fun.

It turns out that imagination provides the best entertainment of all.

Definitions:

1. chicken - cowardly, a bird

2. clothes - garments

3. potato - a root vegetable

4. rough - not smooth

5. monkey - a small animal cousin to apes

6. babies - infants

7. pickle - preserved cucumbers in vinegar

8. nothing - absence of

9. answer - to reply

10. dinosaur - large, extinct reptiles

Creative Writing Page

DOODLE YOUR DEFINITION

DOODLE YOUR DEFINITION

Parent Sheet

Lesson: _____ Date: _____

Activity Used: _____ Fun? Y N

Word List: Mastered? (Circle if not)

1. chicken   ☐
2. clothes   ☐
3. potato   ☐
4. rough   ☐
5. monkey   ☐
6. babies   ☐
7. pickle   ☐
8. nothing   ☐
9. answer   ☐
10. dinosaur   ☐

Notes:

_____

_____

_____

_____

How I am feeling today: 😀 😜 😔 😠 😳 😍 🤨 😖

Parent Check Up

You are ALL done!

In the last 5 lessons, which words or activities did your child enjoy the most? Have your student write or draw their answer here and discuss.

You did it! If your child completed all of the lessons, then they have conquered some of the most commonly misspelled words used in everyday language. It may have seem like very little, but just look at all of the words your wiggly young genius has powered through...

Words Mastered:

1. will	2. too	3. ice
4. two	5. eat	6. who
7. you	8. but	9. ask
10. beg	11. few	12. one
13. ago	14. fly	15. won
16. pony	17. sea	18. does
19. war	20. our	21. why
22. tall	23. ears	24. pull
25. said	26. eyes	27. again
28. don't	29. ugly	30. every
31. back	32. when	33. they
34. each	35. goes	36. know
37. then	38. cube	39. nice
40. rage	41. used	42. sure
43. calm	44. only	45. hurt
46. come	47. okay	48. high
49. road	50. mold	51. boat
52. wait	53. stair	54. hour
55. scary	56. white	57. race
58. oil	59. head	60. sorry
61. many	62. once	63. bear
64. place	65. very	66. hair
67. blue	68. long	69. home

70. made	71. please	72. music
73. wonder	74. dollar	75. threw
76. money	77. blood	78. huge
79. cloud	80. whose	81. gone
82. ninth	83. would	84. coming
85. poison	86. ready	87. police
88. animal	89. actual	90. noise
91. their	92. watch	93. fairy
94. about	95. right	96. daily
97. where	98. large	99. night
100. autumn	101. which	102. sleepy
103. heard	104. great	105. while
106. fourth	107. didn't	108. caught
109. pretty	110. laugh(ed)	111. magical
112. since	113. half	114. awful
115. country	116. fence	117. hospital
118. knife	119. flour	120. flower
121. minutes	122. science	123. field
124. round	125. always	126. whole
127. almost	128. wreck	129. muscle
130. weather	131. sugar	132. juicy
133. heart	134. giant	135. tired
136. buying	137. wives	138. color/colour
139. ghost	140. usually	141. chicken
142. clothes	143. potato	144. rough
145. monkey	146. babies	147. pickle
148. nothing	149. answer	150. dinosaur

THIS IS TO CERTIFY THAT

BRAIN BREAK BOOKS
INSPIRE LEARNING
CELEBRATE DISCOVERY!

DATE

TEACHER

HAS ACHIEVED

★

SPELLING MASTERY!

CERTIFICATE

OF TEACHING
AWESOMENESS

This Certifies that

Is a phenomenal parent who successfully facilitated and delivered a solid teaching program in spelling to a wiggly learner and is deserving of a massage, bubble bath, chocolate or any other treat deemed necessary.

DATE

BRAIN BREAK BOOKS
INSPIRE LEARNING
CELEBRATE DISCOVERY!

PRINCIPAL

WAY TO GO!

This is cause for celebration for you BOTH!
We are so proud of you!
Time for a dollar store treat spree for your spelling master and perhaps a candle lit bubble bath for you!
Who knew spelling could be so fun?
Now; keep it going. Feel free to enjoy a break, but use the ideas here and your own to keep the momentum moving. Here are some helpful lists of more advanced words for your brilliant speller to keep progressing with...

More Spelling Lists:

List 1:
1. enough
2. easiest
3. guess
4. chocolate
5. numb
6. knotted
7. shining
8. breakfast
9. grandma
10. promise

List 2:
1. straight
2. million
3. shelves
4. measure
5. building
6. dessert
7. strange
8. chief
9. though
10. promise

List 3:
1. delicious
2. climbing
3. adventure
4. centuries
5. grocery
6. listening
7. knocked
8. calendar
9. kitchen
10. strawberry

List 4:
1. bicycle
2. questions
3. castle
4. surprise
5. lettuce
6. butterfly
7. intelligent
8. gorgeous
9. restaurant
10. fashion

List 5:
1. piano
2. husband
3. supposed
4. helicopter
5. coffee
6. medicine
7. weird
8. island
9. material
10. character

List 6:
1. popular
2. diamond
3. gigantic
4. foreign
5. ordinary
6. courtesy
7. cough
8. company
9. business
10. princess

List 7:

1. unknown
2. frequently
3. experience
4. address
5. knowledge
6. consciousness
7. rhythm
8. beginning
9. mischief
10. whisper

List 8:

1. weight
2. ballet
3. seizure
4. scientist
5. variety
6. specialty
7. embarrass
8. exaggerate
9. captured
10. soldiers

List 9:

1. battle
2. invisible
3. invincible
4. possibility
5. saddle
6. growing
7. congratulations
8. community
9. enemy
10. trophy

List 10:

1. general
2. departure
3. beautiful
4. going
5. people
6. graduate
7. satisfied
8. makeup
9. motion
10. boundary

List 11:
1. waterfall
2. shoulder
3. volume
4. brilliant
5. conceive
6. opposite
7. opportunity
8. principal
9. principle
10. thieves

List 12:
1. duty
2. possession
3. punctuation
4. process
5. committee
6. discipline
7. vacuum
8. skiing
9. athlete
10. honor/honour

List 13:
1. receive
2. coaches
3. receipt
4. cities
5. cellphone
6. whatever
7. elephant
8. bracelet
9. jewelry/jewellery
10. school

List 14:
1. garbage
2. junior
3. cousin
4. happily
5. aunty
6. dolphin
7. necklace
8. giraffe
9. twelve
10. friend

List 15:
1. families
2. spring
3. violet
4. because
5. whistle
6. tomorrow
7. favorite/favourite
8. frighten
9. necessary
10. appreciate

List 16:
1. kindergarten
2. course
3. orange
4. Wednesday
5. maternity
6. daughter
7. location
8. theater/theatre
9. correction
10. scissors

That should keep you busy for a few weeks yet!

ABOUT THE AUTHORS

Tina Jacobs Ramsay

Tina is a homeschooling wife to her loving husband Curtis and Momma to two amazing children; Tazhae and Isaiah. Her homeschooling journey began with her sons' diagnosis of autism, ADD, dyslexia, dyscalculia and dysgraphia. The school system was failing him and suggested Tina just accept that he was incapable of learning. This preempted the pull from the public system and a lifelong journey to find a better way to educate her unique child in a way that allowed him to excel. She found he is a right brained learner and exceptionally intelligent. Through incorporating movement, embracing picture based learning and allowing his interests to lead their curriculum, Isaiah has developed into a confident public speaker, excited to learn and self motivated in his studies. Tina now offers educational consulting and is making big plans to revolutionize the American educational system with her new fun approach to schooling.

The Ramsays currently live in South Carolina, USA.

Subscribe to Tinas' YouTube channel: **Homeschooling and Oils.**

Shantell Androschuk

Shantell is the widow of Barry and proud mom to four wonderful children; Cheridynn, Éowynn, Atticus and Brigette. A former high school teacher married to a master teacher, both parents were determined to homeschool from day one and allow their children to embrace learning with joy. The four children vary from extremely advanced to severe educational delays and this has precipitated the development of new curriculum that supports all kinds of learners. It is Shantells' hope that Brain Break Books will be the educational spark that makes a whole new generation of thinkers who are ravenous in their pursuit of learning. The Androschuks reside in Alberta, Canada.

Subscribe to her YouTube channel: **Androschuk Academy.**

Amber Masson

Amber is a baking genius, loving wife to Bill and mom to four busy boys; Dirk, Hunter, Tristan and Bowen. Her days are full of slugs, snails and puppy dog tails, complete with lots of laughter. Her tiny moments of quiet show her artistic talent and we are delighted that she was able to gift us with some of her amusing illustrations.
The Massons live in Alberta, Canada.

Brain Break Books

How did you enjoy this book? Any areas we could improve upon?

We would love to here from you!

brainbreakbooks@gmail.com

Watch also for our next two levels:

Kinetic Spelling for Active Learners; Middle School

and

Kinetic Spelling for Active Learners; High School

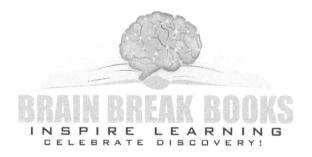

Follow us on our Website:

www.brainbreakbooks.com

Notes:

Notes:

Dear Facilitator:

This program is designed by Educational Professionals with right brained and active learners in mind. This program used words from the most misspelled words in the english language and were selected to present a challenge while also building self esteem. If the activities were followed as written, then this program covered:

Spelling

Comprehension

Reading

Physical Education

Art

Letter Recognition

Writing

Our methods are selected to incorporate the types of short attention spans that often equal a learning difficulty in the focused study of grammatical skills. It is our sincere hope that this helped these "wiggly learners" to find success.

Thank you for your support!

Stay tuned for our Upcoming Titles, available in

Middle and High School level Unit Studies:

CryptoCurrency

30 Unique Horse Breeds

Egyptology

Human Anatomy

Slavery through the Ages

Around the World

and...

MANY MORE!

Check out our website for the most current release dates.

www.brainbreakbooks.com

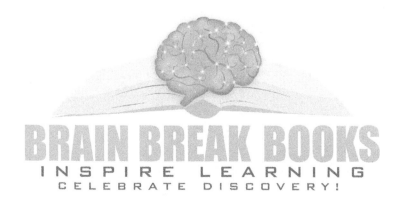

66766143R00104